MATT REDMAN

We Shall Not Be Shaken

EDITOR ANDREW HIGH
ART DESIGN MARC LUDENA
TRANSCRIBER BRYCE INMAN
PRODUCTION COORDINATOR LIZ GEORGE
EXECUTIVE PRODUCER JOHN J. THOMPSON

WORSHIP TOGETHER.com®

TABLE OF CONTENTS

This Is How We Know

Words and Music by
MATT REDMAN and BETH REDMAN

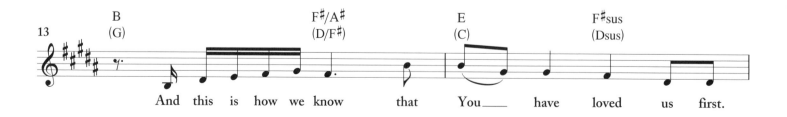

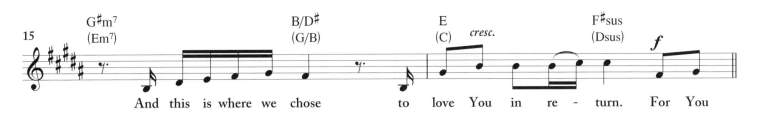

And this is where we chose to love You in re- turn. For You

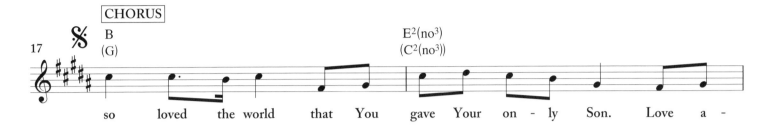

CHORUS

so loved the world that You gave Your on- ly Son. Love a-

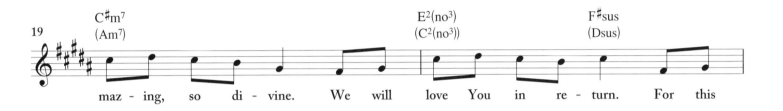

maz- ing, so di- vine. We will love You in re- turn. For this

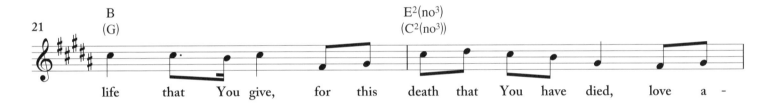

life that You give, for this death that You have died, love a-

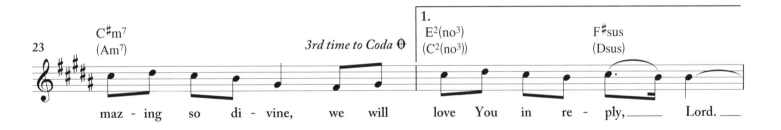

3rd time to Coda

1.

maz- ing so di- vine, we will love You in re- ply,____ Lord. ____

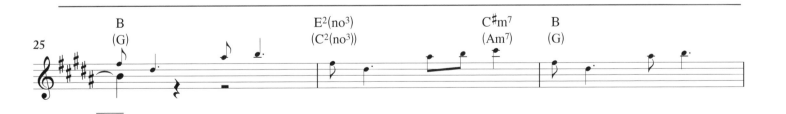

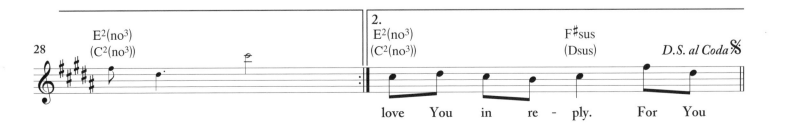

2.

D.S. al Coda

love You in re- ply. For You

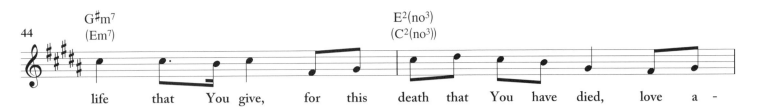

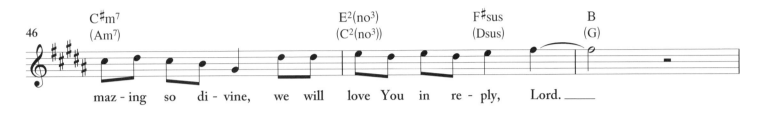

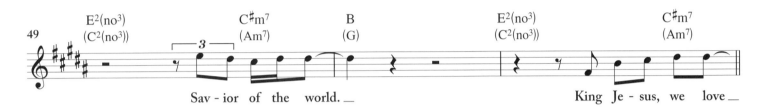

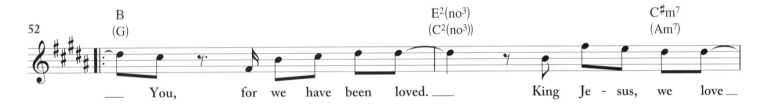

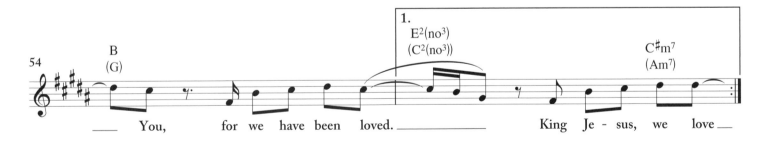

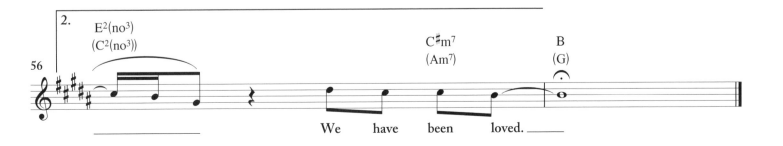

We Shall Not Be Shaken

Words and Music by
MATT REDMAN and JONAS MYRIN

Through It All

Words and Music by
MATT REDMAN and JONAS MYRIN

Capo 4 (G)

Moderate rock beat ♩ = 88

Keyboard (Guitar)

C#m⁷ (Am⁷) G#m⁷ (Em⁷) F# (D) C#m⁷ (Am⁷) G#m⁷ (Em⁷) F# (D)

mf

Through it all __

CHORUS

C#m⁷ (Am⁷) G#m⁷ (Em⁷) F# (D)

__ You __ are faith - ful, through it all __

C#m⁷ (Am⁷) G#m⁷ (Em⁷) F# (D) C#m⁷ (Am⁷) G#m⁷ (Em⁷)

__ You __ are strong. __ As we walk __ through __ the sha -

F# (D) E (C) G#m⁷ (Em⁷) F# (D)

- dows, still You shine on, __ oh. __

VERSE

B (G) F#/A# (D/F#) G#m⁷ (Em⁷) E (C)

1. So man - y bro - ken prom - is - es, __
2. God of un - bro - ken prom - is - es, __

B (G) F#/A# (D/F#) B (G)

so man - y emp - ty words; __ God of love __ and faith -
al - ways You keep __ Your word; __ Glo - ry, grace __ and ho -

F#/A# (D/F#) G#m⁷ (Em⁷) E (C) B (G)

- ful - ness, __ have mer - cy on __ this world.
- li - ness, __ for - ev - er to __ en - dure.

This page has intentionally been left blank.

You Alone Can Rescue

Words and Music by
MATT REDMAN and JONAS MYRIN

Capo 4 (G)

Worshipfully ♩ = 69

VERSE 1

1. Who, O _____ Lord, could save them- selves, their own _ soul could _ heal? Our shame was _ deep - er than the sea. Your grace is deep - er still.

1. still.

2. still.

CHORUS

And You a - lone can res - cue, You a - lone can save. You a - lone can lift us from _ the grave. _ You came down to find us, led us out of

BRIDGE

39

B
(G)

E²(no³)
(C²(no³))

___ up our eyes, lift ___ up our eyes. You're the giv - er of life. We lift ___

41

B
(G)

E²(no³)
(C²(no³))

___ up our eyes, lift ___ up our eyes. You're the giv - er of life. We lift ___

43

G♯m⁷
(Em⁷)

E²(no³)
(C²(no³))

___ up our eyes, lift ___ up our eyes. You're the giv - er of life. We lift ___

45

G♯m⁷
(Em⁷)

1.
E²(no³)
(C²(no³))

___ up our eyes, lift ___ up our eyes. You're the giv - er of life. We lift ___

2.

47

E²(no³)
(C²(no³))

mp

CHORUS

E
(C)

F♯sus
(Dsus)

giv - er of life. And You a - lone can res - cue, You a - lone can

50

G♯m⁷
(Em⁷)

E
(C)

F♯sus
(Dsus)

G♯m⁷
(Em⁷)

save. You a - lone can lift us from ___ the grave. ___ You came down to

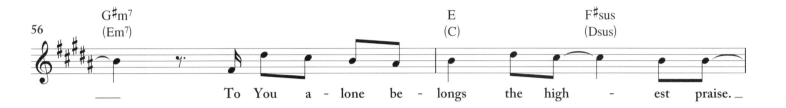

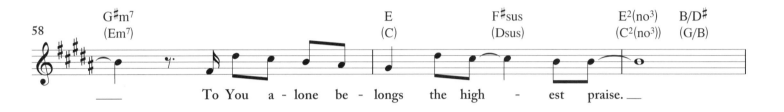

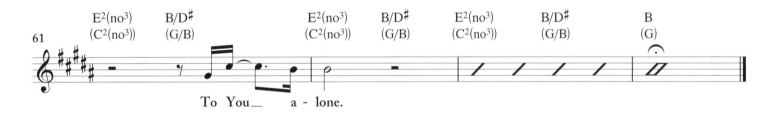

The Glory of Our King

Words and Music by
JONAS MYRIN, JESS CATES
and MATT REDMAN

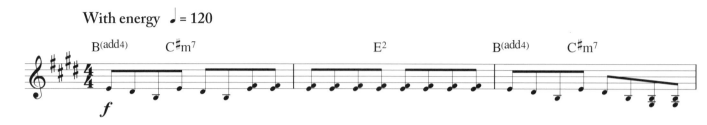

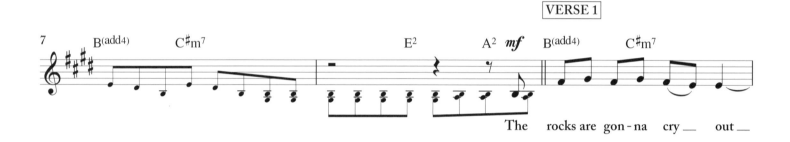

VERSE 1

The rocks are gon-na cry ___ out

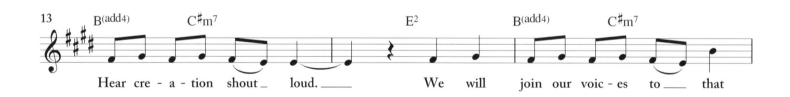

___ if we don't. Now's the time to raise ___ a song.

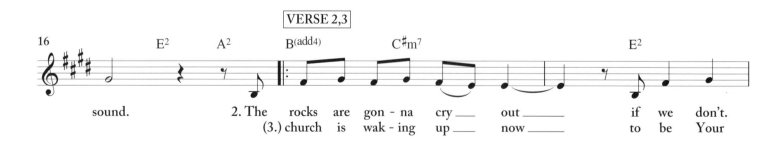

Hear cre-a-tion shout ___ loud. ___ We will join our voic-es to ___ that

VERSE 2,3

sound.   2. The rocks are gon-na cry ___ out ___ if we don't.
(3.) church is wak-ing up ___ now ___ to be Your

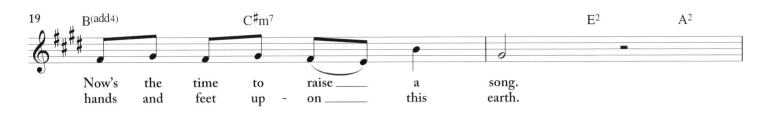

Now's the time to raise ___ a song.
hands and feet up-on ___ this earth.

Hear cre-a-tion shout ___ loud. ___ We will
Send us in Your pow - er ___ as we take

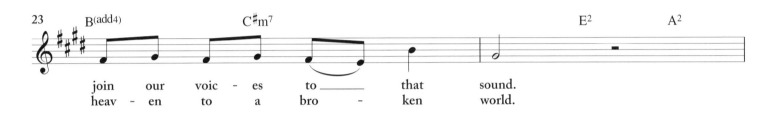

join our voic-es to ___ that sound.
heav-en to a bro-ken world.

CHORUS

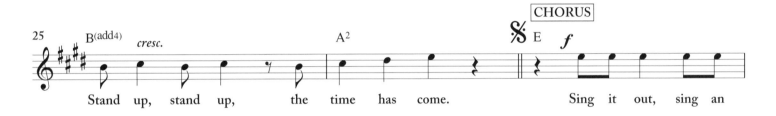

Stand up, stand up, the time has come. Sing it out, sing an

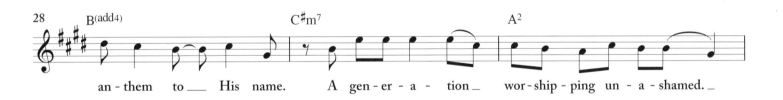

an-them to ___ His name. A gen-er-a-tion ___ wor-ship-ping un-a-shamed. ___

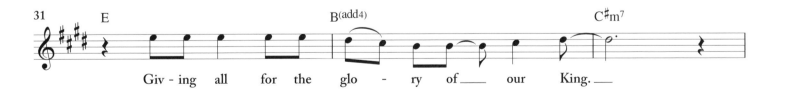

Giv-ing all for the glo - ry of ___ our King. ___

We will run, we will run af-ter ___ Your heart.

We be - lieve You are all that You say You are. ___

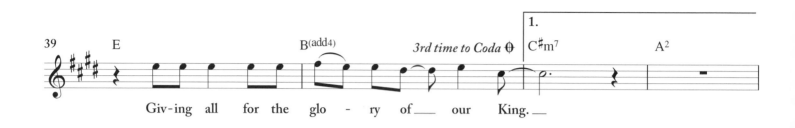

Giv-ing all for the glo - ry of ___ our King. ___

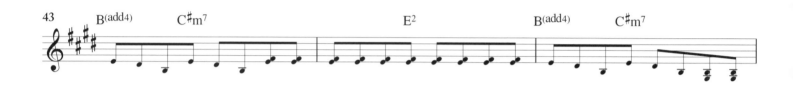

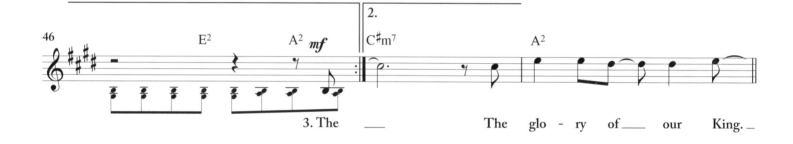

3. The ___ The glo - ry of ___ our King. ___

___ The glo - ry of ___ our King. ___

___

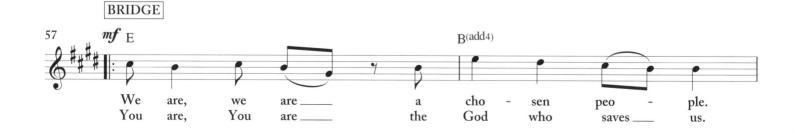

BRIDGE

We are, we are ___ a cho - sen peo - ple.
You are, You are ___ the God who saves ___ us.

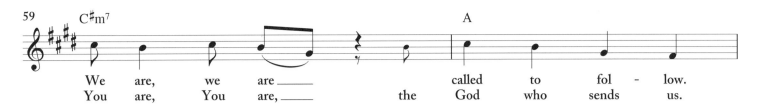

We are, we are _____ the called to fol - low.
You are, You are, _____ the God who sends us.

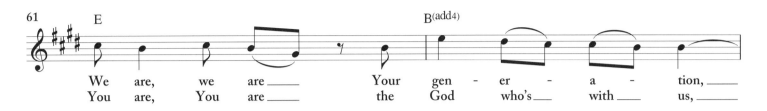

We are, we are _____ Your gen - er - a - tion, _____
You are, You are _____ the God who's ___ with ___ us, _____

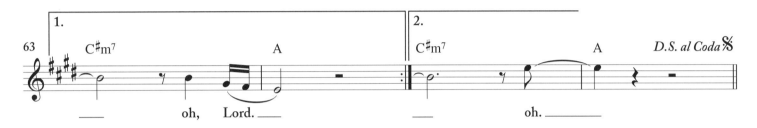

1.
_____ oh, Lord. ___

2.
D.S. al Coda
_____ oh. _____

CODA

TAG

2nd time: vocal ad lib.

___ The glo - ry of ___ our King. _____

It's all for the glo - ry of ___ our King. _____

1.

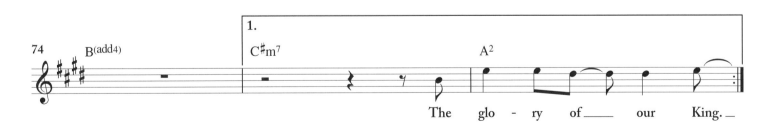

The glo - ry of ___ our King. ___

2.

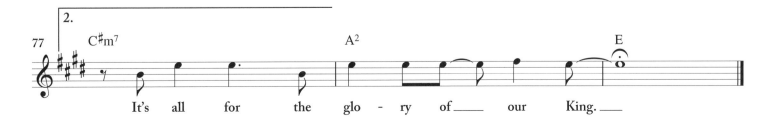

It's all for the glo - ry of ___ our King. _____

How Great Is Your Faithfulness

Words and Music by
JONAS MYRIN and MATT REDMAN

Capo 4 (G)

Remembrance (Communion Song)

Words and Music by
MATT MAHER and MATT REDMAN

The More We See

Words and Music by
MATT REDMAN and CHRIS TOMLIN

Moderate rock beat ♩ = 88

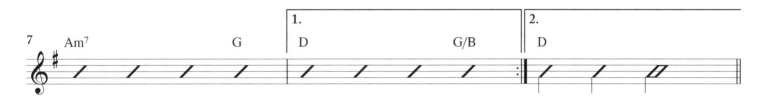

VERSE

1. Our hearts __ are breath - ing in __ the won - ders of __ Your name, __
2. Your pow'r __ we see __ dis - played __ in all __ the You __ have made __

and we're breath - ing out __ Your praise. __
in the sky __ and sea __ and stars. __

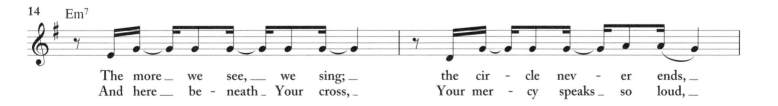

The more __ we see, __ we sing; __ the cir - cle nev - er ends, __
And here __ be - neath Your cross, __ Your mer - cy speaks so loud, __

for Your glo - ry nev - er fades. ___ And
speak - ing straight ___ in - to ___ our hearts. ___

chords in parentheses 2nd time only:

sure - ly as the ris - ing ___ sun, _____ Your

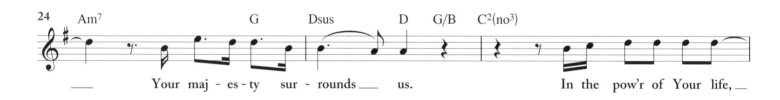

love, O Lord, en - dures, Your love en - dures for - ev - er.

CHORUS

From the heights of Your throne ___ to the depths of Your heart, ___

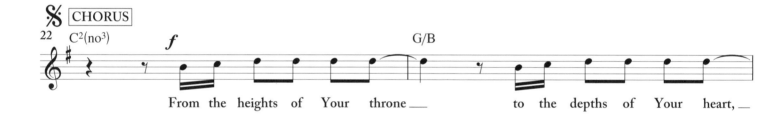

___ Your maj - es - ty sur - rounds ___ us. In the pow'r of Your life, ___

3rd time to Coda

___ in the grace of Your cross, ___ Your mer - cy, Lord, has found ___ us.

found _____ us. Oh, Lord.

found ____ us. And the more we see, we sing, "Ho - ly is the name of ____

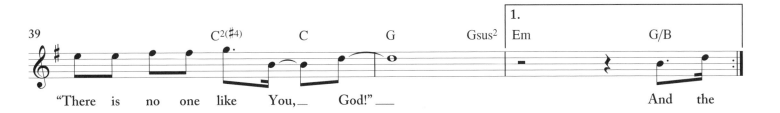

____ the Lord!" ____ And the more we see, we sing,

"There is no one like You,__ God!" ____ And the

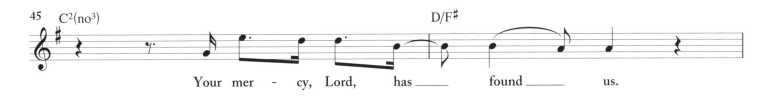

Your maj - es - ty sur - rounds ____ us, oh.

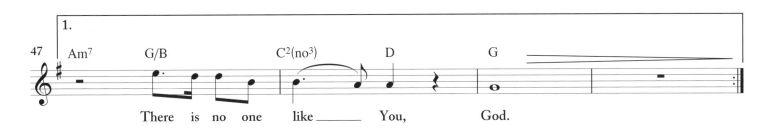

Your mer - cy, Lord, has ____ found ____ us.

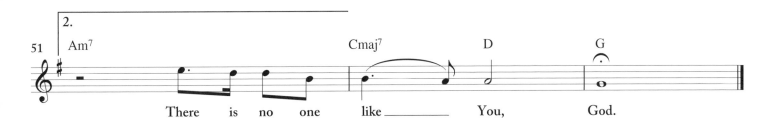

There is no one like ____ You, God.

There is no one like ____ You, God.

For Your Glory

Words and Music by
BEN CANTELON and MATT REDMAN

Gloria

Words and Music by
JONAS MYRIN, MATT REDMAN
and PETER KVINT

All That Really Matters

Words and Music by
JONAS MYRIN and MATT REDMAN

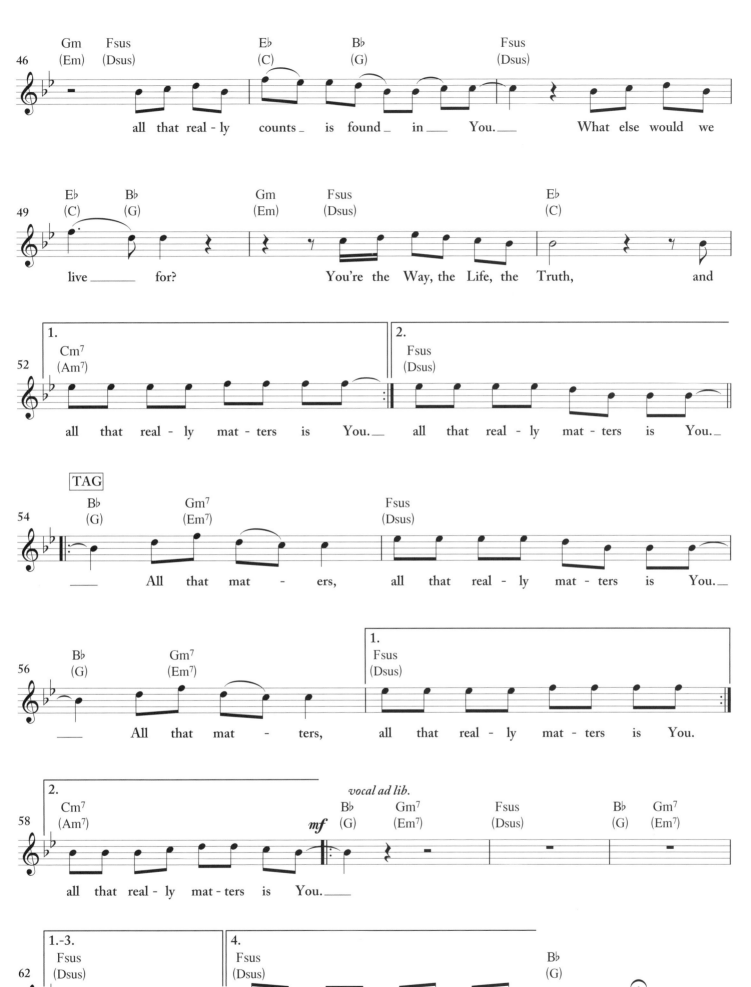

My Hope

Words and Music by
TIM WANSTALL and MATT REDMAN

- ing, I shall be safe in You.___ Though the na - tions are quak-

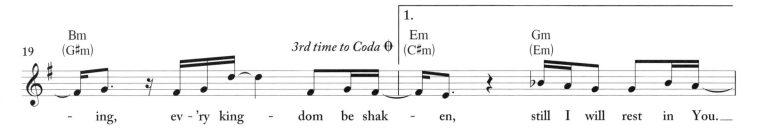

- ing, ev-'ry king - dom be shak - en, still I will rest in You.___

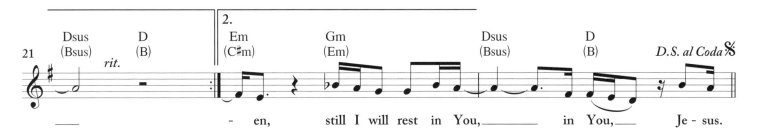

___ - en, still I will rest in You,_____ in You,___ Je - sus.

θ CODA

- en, still I will rest in You.___

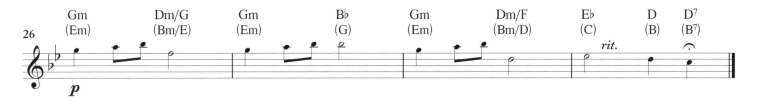

THIS IS HOW WE KNOW

MATT REDMAN and BETH REDMAN

KEY OF (B)

G	C²(no³)	Am⁷	C	Dsus	D/F♯	Em⁷	G/B	G²	D

Capo 4 (G)

G   C²(no³)   Am⁷   G   C²(no³)

VERSE:

G
   This is how we know,

This is how we know what love is:
C   Dsus
   Just one look at Your cross.
     G
And this is where we see,

This is where we see how love works,
C   Dsus
   For You surrendered Your all.
G   D/F♯
   And this is how we know
     C   Dsus
That You have loved us first.
Em⁷   G/B
     And this is where we chose
    C   Dsus
To love You in re - turn.

CHORUS:
     G
For You so loved the world
      C²(no³)
That You gave Your only Son.
     Am⁷
Love a - mazing, so divine.
      C²(no³)   Dsus
We will love You in re - turn.
     G
For this life that You give,
      C²(no³)
For this death that You have died,
     Am⁷
Love a - mazing so divine,
      C²(no³)   Dsus
We will love You in re - ply, Lord.

CONTINUED...

G   C²(no³)   Am⁷   G   C²(no³)

(repeat VERSE)

(repeat CHORUS twice)

BRIDGE:
                  C   D/F♯
And our love will be loud, our love will be strong.
                Am⁷
Our love should be hands and feet
     G²   Dsus   G
That serve You in   this world.
                 C   G/B
So, let it stay true, and let it en - dure,
              Am⁷   D
That You will be glorified worshipped and adored.

(repeat CHORUS)

G   C²(no³)   Am⁷   G   C²(no³)
           Savior of the world.

TAG:
        Am⁷   G
King Jesus, we love   You,
                   C²(no³)
For we have been loved.
        Am⁷   G
King Jesus, we love   You,
                     C²(no³)
For we have been loved.

(repeat TAG)

        Am⁷   G
We have been loved.

WE SHALL NOT BE SHAKEN

MATT REDMAN and JONAS MYRIN

KEY OF (F)

Bm   A   G   D   F#m⁷   D/F#   A/C#

Capo 3 (D)

INTRO:

Bm A G A Bm A G A

VERSE:

```
                Bm
When everything's breaking,
 A            G
   You are left un - shaken.
 A              Bm
   When everything's tumbling down,
 A            G
You're the solid ground.
 A            Bm      A       G
   Nations could be quaking,    economies failing,
 A            Bm
   When fear is found all around,
 A            G      A
You're the solid ground.
```

CHORUS:

```
          D   F#m⁷       G        D
Our God, You are      all that You say You are.
       Bm            D/F#        G
You never change, You never fail,   You never fade.
          D   F#m⁷       G        D
Our God, You are      faithful in all Your ways.
       Bm            D/F#        G
Forever You stand, forever You reign, forever re-main.
      N.C.
And we shall not be shaken.
```

1st time only:

```
Bm A G A                    Bm A G A
   We shall not be shaken.
```

(REPEAT VERSE)

(REPEAT CHORUS)

CONTINUED...

BRIDGE:

```
D/F#
We shall, we shall not be shaken.
G
We shall, we shall not be shaken.
           D          A/C#
When all around is sinking sand.
      D/F#
For You are, You are never changing.
G
You are, You are never changing.
D          A/C#
You will stand, the great I AM, Lord.
```

(REPEAT BRIDGE)

The great I AM.

(REPEAT CHORUS)

TAG:

```
                   D
Our God, You are,
 F#m⁷                    A        D
      You are all that You say You are.
       Bm            D/F#         G
You never change, You never fail,   You never fade.
          D  F#m⁷      G        D
Our God, You are      faithful in all Your ways.
       Bm            D/F#
Forever You stand, forever You reign,
             G
Forever re - main.

And we shall not be shaken,
            N.C.
We shall not be shaken.
```

THROUGH IT ALL
MATT REDMAN and JONAS MYRIN

KEY OF (B)

Am⁷ Em⁷ D C D/F♯ G Dm Em G/B Am Cm

Capo 4 (G)

INTRO:

Am⁷ Em⁷ D Am⁷ Em⁷ D

        Am⁷ Em⁷   D
Through it all   You   are faith - ful,
        Am⁷ Em⁷   D
Through it all   You   are strong.
        Am⁷ Em⁷   D
As we walk   through   the sha - dows,
           C Em⁷ D
Still You shine on,   oh.

VERSE 1:

G   D/F♯ Em⁷   C
So many broken prom - is - es,
G   D/F♯
So many empty words;
G   D/F♯ Em⁷   C
God of love and faith - ful - ness,
     G   D/F♯
Have mercy on this world.
         Dm   C
You never turn   or change.
         Cm   G/B
You never break   the faith.
Dm   C
Yesterday, today and always.

CHORUS:

        Bm Em⁷   D
Through it all   You   are faith - ful,
        Bm Em⁷   D
Through it all   You   are strong.
        Bm Em⁷   D
As we walk   through   the sha - dows,
           C Em⁷
Still You shine on,

CONTINUED...

1st, 3rd amd 4th times only:

D   G Em⁷ D
  Still You shine on.

1st time go to VERSE 2.
2nd and 3rd times go to BRIDGE

VERSE 2:

G   D/F♯ Em⁷   C
God of unbroken prom - is - es,
G   D/F♯
Always You keep Your word;
G   D/F♯ Em⁷   C
Glory, grace and ho - li - ness,
         G   D/F♯
For - ever to endure.
         Dm   C
You never turn   or change.
         Cm   G/B
You never break   the faith.
Dm   C
Yesterday, today and always.

(REPEAT CHORUS twice)

BRIDGE:

        C G D   Bm Em⁷   D
You are faith - ful, Jesus, You are faithful to the end.
        C G D   Bm Em⁷   D
You are faith - ful. Jesus, You are faithful to the end.

(REPEAT CHORUS)

TAG:

         Dm   C
You never turn   or change.
         Cm   G
You never break   the faith.

YOU ALONE CAN RESCUE

MATT REDMAN and JONAS MYRIN

KEY OF (B)

C²(no³) Dsus Em⁷ G C D G/B Gsus

INTRO:
Capo 4 (G)

C²(no³)   Dsus   Em⁷   C²(no³)   Dsus

VERSE 1:
GG   C   G
Who, O Lord, could save them - selves,
C   Dsus   E
Their own soul could heal?
  Em⁷   G/B C   G
Our shame was deeper than the sea.
  C   Dsus   G
Your grace is deeper still.

(REPEAT VERSE 1)

CHORUS:
     C   Dsus   Em⁷
And You alone can rescue, You alone can save.
     C   Dsus   Em⁷
You alone can lift us from   the grave.
     C   Dsus   Em⁷
You came down to find us, led us out of death.
    C   E
To You alone be-longs the high - est praise.
1st time only: Gsus G

VERSE 2:
    C   G
You, O Lord, have made a way.
  C   Dsus   E
The great divide, You healed.
  Em⁷ G/B   C   G
For when our hearts were far a-way,
   C   Dsus   G
Your love went further still.
    C   Dsus   G
Yes, Your love goes further still.

(REPEAT CHORUS)

CONTINUED...

Em⁷ G   C   E
To You alone be-longs the hig - hest praise.
G Gsus G Gsus G   Gsus G Gsus
You alone.

BRIDGE:
     G
We lift up our eyes, lift up our eyes.
      C²(no³)
You're the giver of life.
     G
We lift up our eyes, lift up our eyes.
      C²(no³)
You're the giver of life.
     Em⁷
We lift   up our eyes, lift up our eyes.
      C²(no³)
You're the giver of life.
     Em⁷
We lift   up our eyes, lift up our eyes.
      C²(no³)
You're the giver of life.

(REPEAT BRIDGE)

(REPEAT CHORUS)

TAG:
Em⁷   C   Dsus   Em⁷
To You alone be-longs the high - est praise.
     C   Dsus
To You alone be-longs the high - est praise.
C²(no³) G/B C²(no³) G/B

     C²(no³) G/B C²(no³) G/B G
To You a-lone.

THE GLORY OF OUR KING

JONAS MYRIN, JESS CATES and MATT REDMAN

KEY OF (E)

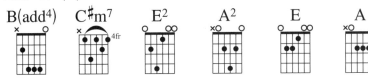

B(add4)   C♯m⁷   E²   A²   E   A

INTRO:
B(add4) C♯m⁷ E² B(add4) C♯m⁷ E² A²
B(add4) C♯m⁷ E² B(add4) C♯m⁷ E² A²

VERSE 1:
    B(add4)   C♯m⁷   E²
The rocks are gon - na cry out if we don't.
B(add4)   C♯m⁷   E²   A²
Now's the time to raise a song.
B(add4)   C♯m⁷   E²
Hear crea - tion shout loud.
      B(add4)   C♯m⁷   E²   A²
We will join our voic - es to that sound.

(REPEAT VERSE 1)

B(add4)   A²
Stand up, stand up, the time has come.

CHORUS:
E   B(add4)
    Sing it out, sing an anthem to His name.
C♯m⁷   A²
      A generation worshipping unashamed.
E   B(add4)   C♯m⁷ A²
    Giving all for the glory of our King.
E   B(add4)
    We will run, we will run after Your heart.
C♯m⁷   A²
      We believe You are all that You say You are.
E   B(add4)   C♯m⁷
    Giving all for the glory of our King.

2nd time go to 2nd Ending, 3rd time to go TAG

1st time only:

A² B(add4) C♯m⁷ E² B(add4) C♯m⁷ E² A²

VERSE 2
    B(add4)   C♯m⁷
The church is wak - ing up now
E²   B(add4)   C♯m⁷   E² A²
To be Your hands and feet upon this earth.

CONTINUED...

B(add4)   C♯m⁷
Send us in Your power
E²   B(add4)   C♯m⁷   E² A²
As we take heaven to a broken world.

(REPEAT CHORUS)

(2nd Ending)

    A²   E B(add4) C♯m⁷
The glory of our King.
    A²   E B(add4) C♯m⁷ A²
The glory of our King.

BRIDGE:
E   B(add4)
We are, we are a chosen people.
C♯m⁷   A
We are, we are called to follow.
E   B(add4)   C♯m⁷   A
We are, we are Your generation,   oh, Lord.
E   B(add4)
You are, You are the God who saves us.
C♯m⁷   A
You are, You are, the God who sends us.
E   B(add4)   C♯m⁷ A
You are, You are the God who's with us, oh.

TAG:
    A²   E B(add4)
The glory of the King.
C♯m⁷   A²   E B(add4)
    It's all for the glory of our King.
C♯m⁷   A²   E B(add4)
    The glory of our King.
        A²   E B(add4)
It's all for the glory of our King.
C♯m⁷   A²   E
The glory of our King.

HOW GREAT IS YOUR FAITHFULNESS
JONAS MYRIN and MATT REDMAN

KEY OF (B)

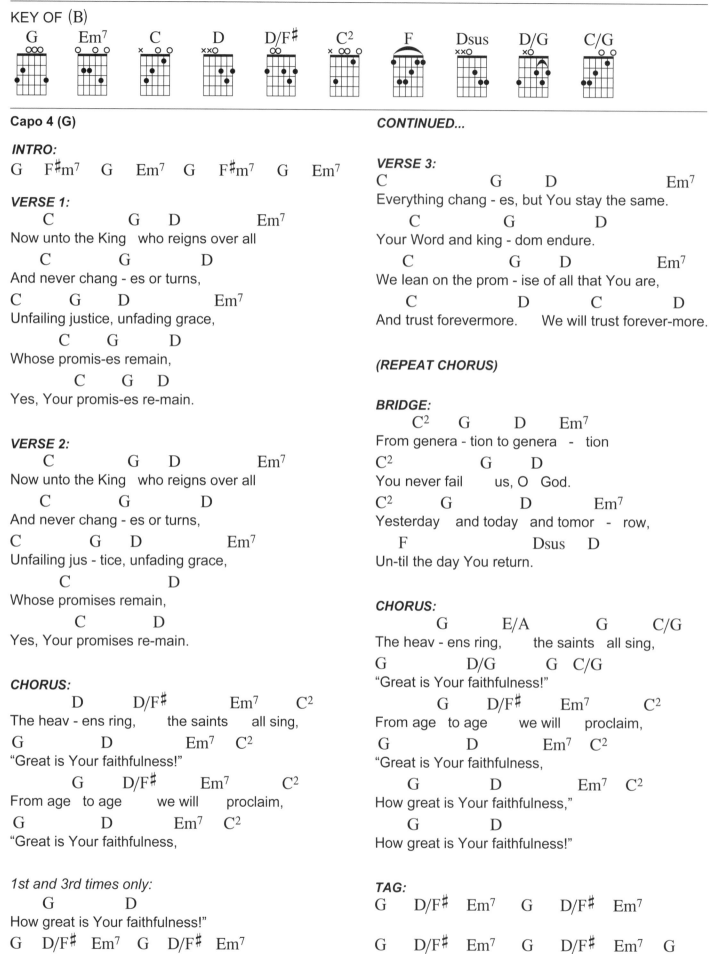

Capo 4 (G)

INTRO:

G   F#m^7 G   Em^7 G   F#m^7 G   Em^7

VERSE 1:

     C   G D   Em^7
Now unto the King who reigns over all
     C   G   D
And never chang - es or turns,
C   G   D   Em^7
Unfailing justice, unfading grace,
       C   G   D
Whose promis-es remain,
         C   G   D
Yes, Your promis-es re-main.

VERSE 2:

     C   G D   Em^7
Now unto the King who reigns over all
     C   G   D
And never chang - es or turns,
C   G   D   Em^7
Unfailing jus - tice, unfading grace,
       C   D
Whose promises remain,
        C   D
Yes, Your promises re-main.

CHORUS:

       D   D/F#   Em^7 C^2
The heav - ens ring,   the saints   all sing,
G   D   Em^7 C^2
"Great is Your faithfulness!"
      G   D/F#   Em^7 C^2
From age to age   we will   proclaim,
G   D   Em^7 C^2
"Great is Your faithfulness,

1st and 3rd times only:
    G   D
How great is Your faithfulness!"
G D/F# Em^7 G D/F# Em^7

CONTINUED...

VERSE 3:

C   G   D   Em^7
Everything chang - es, but You stay the same.
      C   G   D
Your Word and king - dom endure.
      C   G   D   Em^7
We lean on the prom - ise of all that You are,
      C   D   C   D
And trust forevermore.   We will trust forever-more.

(REPEAT CHORUS)

BRIDGE:

     C^2 G   D   Em^7
From genera - tion to genera - tion
C^2 G   D
You never fail   us, O God.
C^2 G   D   Em^7
Yesterday   and today and tomor - row,
    F   Dsus   D
Un-til the day You return.

CHORUS:

       G   E/A   G   C/G
The heav - ens ring,   the saints   all sing,
G   D/G   G   C/G
"Great is Your faithfulness!"
      G   D/F#   Em^7 C^2
From age to age   we will   proclaim,
G   D   Em^7 C^2
"Great is Your faithfulness,
      G   D   Em^7 C^2
How great is Your faithfulness,"
     G   D
How great is Your faithfulness!"

TAG:

G D/F# Em^7 G D/F# Em^7

G D/F# Em^7 G D/F# Em^7 G

REMEMBRANCE (COMMUNION SONG)
MATT MAHER and MATT REDMAN

KEY OF (E♭)

D   Dmaj⁷   Em⁷   D/F♯   G²   A   Bm⁷   G   Bm

Capo 1 (D)

INTRO:

D   Dmaj⁷   Em⁹   D   Dmaj⁷   Em⁹

VERSE 1:

    D
Oh, how could it be that my
Dmaj⁷   Em⁹
God would welcome me in-to this mystery,
           D
Say, "Take this bread, take this, wine"?
      Dmaj⁷   Em⁹
Now the simple made divine for any to receive.
        D/F♯   G²   A
By Your mer - cy we come   to Your ta - ble.
           Em⁹   D/F♯   G²
By Your grace   You are mak - ing us faith - ful.

CHORUS:
           D   Bm⁷   A
Lord, we re - mem - ber You,
       G²   D   A
And remem - brance leads   us to wor - ship.
       G²   D   A
And as we wor - ship You,
       G²   D   A   *3rd time*
Our wor - ship leads   to commun - ion.   *to TAG*
          Em⁷   D/F♯   G²
We respond   to Your   invita - tion.
2nd time: (Bm   A)
        A   D   *1st time:* Dmaj⁷   Em⁹
We re - mem - ber   You.

VERSE 2:
       D
See His body, His blood;
       Dmaj⁷   Em⁹
Know that He has overcome every trial we will face.
        D
And none too lost to be saved,
       Dmaj⁷
None too broken or ashamed.
        Em⁹
All are welcome in this place.

CONTINUED...

         D/F♯   G²   A
By Your mer - cy we come   to Your ta - ble.
          Em⁹   D/F♯   G²
By Your grace   You are mak - ing us faith - ful.

(REPEAT CHORUS)

BRIDGE:
           G   A   D
Dying, You de - stroyed our   death.
          G   A   Bm⁷
Rising, You re - stored our   life.
               A
Lord Jesus, come in glory.
             G   D
Lord Jesus, come in glory.

(REPEAT BRIDGE)
               D
Lord Jesus, come in glory.
Dmaj⁷   Em⁹
           Jeus, come.
         D/F♯   D²   A
By Your mer - cy we come   to Your ta - ble.
          Em⁹   D/F♯   G²
By Your grace   You are mak - ing us faith - ful.

(REPEAT CHORUS)

TAG
          Em⁷   D/F♯   G²
We respond   to Your   invita - tion.
          Em⁷   D/F♯   G²
We respond   to Your   invita - tion.
          Bm   A   D
We re - mem - ber   You.

THE MORE WE SEE

MATT REDMAN and CHRIS TOMLIN

KEY OF (G)

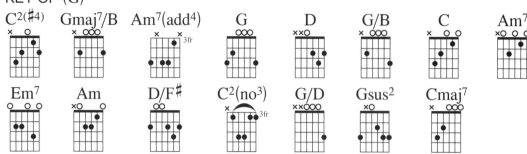

INTRO:

C²(♯4)   Gmaj⁷/B   Am⁷(add⁴)   G   D   G/B

C   G/B   Am⁷   G   D   G/B

C   G/B   Am⁷   G   D

VERSE 1:

Em⁷
   Our hearts are breathing in

The wonders of Your name,
C
   And we're breathing out Your praise.
Em⁷
   The more we see, we sing;

The circle never ends,
C
   For Your glory never fades.
  Am   Em
And surely as the rising sun,
   C
Your love, O Lord, endures,
  Am⁷   G/B
Your love endures forev - er.

CHORUS:

C²(no³)   G/B
   From the heights of Your throne
            Am⁷
To the depths of Your heart,
       G   Dsus D G/B
Your majes - ty sur - rounds us.
C²(no³)   G/B
   In the power of Your life,
            Am⁷
In the grace of Your cross,

CONTINUED...

        G   Dsus   D
Your mercy, Lord, has found us.

1st time only: C   G/B   Am⁷

VERSE 2:

Em⁷
   Your power we see displayed

In all the You have made
C
   In the sky and sea and stars.
Em⁷
   And here beneath Your cross,

Your mercy speaks so loud,
C
   Speaking straight into our hearts.
  Am   Em D/F♯ G G/B
And surely as the rising sun,
   C
Your love, O Lord, endures,
  Am⁷   G/B
Your love endures forev - er.

(REPEAT CHORUS twice)

BRIDGE:

      C
And the more we see, we sing,
        C²(♯4) C G   G⁴₂
"Holy is the name   of the Lord!"
Em⁷ G/B C
   And the more we see, we sing,
        C²(♯4) C   Em G/B
"There is no one like You, God!"

CONTINUED...

Am⁷   G/B

       Your majesty sur - rounds us, oh.

$C^2(no^3)$ D/F♯

         Your mercy, Lord,   has found us.

Am⁷   G/B $C^2(no^3)$ D   G

       There is no one like   You, God.

Am⁷   G/B

       Your majesty sur - rounds us, oh.

$C^2(no^3)$ D/F♯

         Your mercy, Lord,   has found us.

Am⁷   G/B   Cmaj⁷   D   G

       There is no one like   You, God.

FOR YOUR GLORY

BEN CANTELON and MATT REDMAN

KEY OF (B)

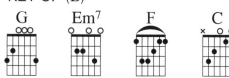

Capo 4 (G)

INTRO:

G   Em⁷   F   C

VERSE 1:

       G

We will dance,   we will dance for Your glory.

We will dance, we will dance for Your glory.

         F   C   G

We will dance   for Your glo - ry, Lord.

VERSE 2:

       G

We will lift   up a shout to adore You.

Every sound that we make, it is for You.

        F   C   G

We will dance   for Your glo - ry, Lord.

CHANNEL:

       A

For salva - tion's in this place.

         C   G

You're the name by which we're saved, Jesus, Jesus!

          F

Let Your name   be lifted high

       C   Em⁷   F

As our thank - ful hearts now cry: Jesus,   Jesus!

CHORUS:

  G

Lift   up your heads, you ancient gates,

  Em⁷

Be   lifted up, You ancient doors.

   F   C

The King is coming in, the King is coming in.

     G

We lift   up a shout to shake the skies,

   Em⁷

Lift   up a cry: be glorified!

   F   C

The King is coming in, the King is coming in.

CONTINUED...

(REPEAT VERSE 1)

(REPEAT CHANNEL)

(REPEAT CHORUS)

G

   King of glory.

BRIDGE

We're the people of God with a song to sing,

And we're bringing our lives as an offering.

        F   C   G

We will dance   for Your glo - ry, Lord.

And Your cross is a hope that we hold up high

As we tell the whole world of Your love and life.

        F   C   G

We will dance   for Your glo - ry, Lord.

(REPEAT CHORUS)

(REPEAT VERSE 1)

(REPEAT VERSE 2)

BRIDGE

G

We're the people of God with a song to sing,

And we're bringing our lives as an offering.

        F   C   G

We will dance   for Your glo - ry, Lord.

        F   C

And Your cross is a hope that we hold up high

        G

As we tell the whole world of Your love and life.

        F   C   G

We will dance   for Your glo - ry, Lord.

GLORIA

JONAS MYRIN, MATT REDMAN and PETER KVINT

KEY OF (D)

| D | A | F♯m⁷ | Esus | A/C♯ | E | C♯m⁷ | B⁷ |

INTRO:

D A F♯m⁷ Esus D A F♯m⁷ Esus

VERSE 1:

A
The skies are filled with Your glory,

D
The oceans mirror Your grace.

      A   D
How deep, how high, how wonderful You are.

A
The earth is telling Your mystery,

D
The heavens sing Your praise.

     F♯m⁷
How deep,   how high, how wonderful

     D
You are,   You are.

    A/C♯   D
We're living to tell Your sto-ry now,

    A/C♯   D   E
Your glory and grace, O God.

CHORUS:

D A F♯m⁷ E
Glori - a!   Glori - a!

D   A   C♯m⁷   F♯m
Heaven and earth sing how great You are.

D A F♯m⁷ E   D
Glori - a!   Glori - a to You evermore!

VERSE 2:

A
The nails and thorns are the offering

D
As You surrendered Your breath.

     F♯m⁷   D
How deep,   how high, how wonderful You are.

A
Now we're becoming an offering,

D
Singing with every last breath.

CONTINUED...

    F♯m⁷
How deep,   how high, how wonderful

     D
You are,   You are.

    A/C♯   D
We're living to tell Your sto-ry now,

    A/C♯   D   E
Your glory and grace, O God.

(REPEAT CHORUS)

A F♯m⁷ E

BRIDGE:

    D   E   F♯m⁷   E
And Yours is the kingdom and the power and the glory,

D   E   F♯m⁷   E
Yours is the anthem and the honor and the story.

Gloria! Gloria! Heaven and earth sing how great You are.

CHORUS:

D A F♯m⁷ E
Glori - a!   Glori - a!

D   A   C♯m⁷   F♯m⁷
Heaven and earth sing how great You are.

D A F♯m⁷ E
Glori - a!   Glori - a!

D   A   C♯m⁷   F♯m⁷
Heaven and earth sing how great You are.

D A F♯m⁷ E   D
Glori - a!   Glori - a to You evermore!

              B⁷   D   A
To You evermore!   Glori - a!

ALL THAT REALLY MATTERS

JONAS MYRIN and MATT REDMAN

KEY OF (B♭)

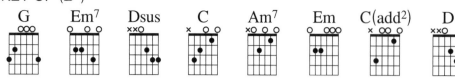

G   Em⁷   Dsus   C   Am⁷   Em   C(add²)   D

Capo 3 (G)

INTRO:

G   Em⁷   Dsus   G   Em⁷   Dsus   *(Repeat)*

VERSE 1:

       G   Em⁷   Dsus
Let our lives   be-come a song   for You,
       G   Em⁷   Dsus
Like a prayer   that reaches high.
  Em⁷   C   Bm⁷   Dsus
The glory of Your name   our greatest cause.

VERSE 2:

       G   Dsus
Let our lives become an of - fering,
       G   Em⁷   Dsus
Ever-pleas - ing to   Your heart.
  Em⁷   C   Am⁷ Dsus
The glory of Your name   our highest call.

CHORUS 1:

       C G   Em Dsus
All that really mat - ters,
        C   G   Dsus
All that really counts is found in You.
          C G   Em
What else would we live   for?
      Dsus   C
You're the Way, the Life, the Truth,
  Am⁷   G Em⁷ Dsus
And all that really matters is You.
        G   Em⁷ Dsus
Jesus, it's You.

VERSE 3:

       G   Dsus
Let our lives become a light   for You,
    C   Em⁷   Dsus
Like a cit - y on   a hill.
  Em⁷   C   Am⁷ Dsus
We'll glorify Your name forevermore.

CONTINUED...

(REPEAT CHORUS):

BRIDGE:
Em⁷   C²
King of glory, be the center.
G   D
King of glory, You'll be the prize.
Em⁷   C²
We shall have no other treasure.
C   D
All that counts is You lifted high.

(REPEAT BRIDGE):

CHORUS 2:
           C G   Em Dsus
All that really mat - ters,
           C   G   Dsus
All that really counts is found in You.
              C G   Em
What else would we live   for?
         Dsus   C
You're the Way, the Life, the Truth,
    Am⁷   G
And all that really matters is You.

(REPEAT CHORUS 2):

TAG:
G   Em⁷   Dsus
  All that matters, all that really matters is You.
G   Em⁷   Dsus
  All that matters, all that really matters is You.
G   Em⁷   Dsus
  All that matters, all that really matters is You.
Am⁷
All that really matters is You.
G   Em⁷ Dsus G   Em⁷ Dsus *(3 times)*

Dsus   G
All that really matters is You.

MY HOPE
TIM WANSTALL and MATT REDMAN

KEY OF (B♭)

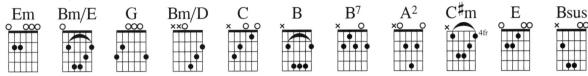

Em Bm/E G Bm/D C B B⁷ A² C♯m E Bsus

Capo 3 (G)

CONTINUED...

INTRO:

Em Bm/E Em G Em Bm/D C B B⁷

(REPEAT CHORUS twice)

VERSE:

   Em   Bm/E   Em   G
My hope is built   on nothing less
Em   Bm/D   C
   Than Jesus' blood and righteousness.
Em   Bm/E   Em   G
   I dare not trust   the sweetest frame,
Em   Bm/D   C   B B⁷
   But wholly lean   on Jesus' name.

Em Bm/E Em G Em Bm/D C B B⁷

CHORUS:

A²   G♯m
   When the mountains are fall - ing,
                 C♯m
When the waters are ris - ing,
E   B
I shall be safe in You.
A²   G♯m
   Though the nations are quak - ing,
               C♯m
Every kingdom be shak - en,
Em   Bsus   B
Still I will rest in You.

VERSE 2:

Em   Bm/E   Em   G
   When darkness seems   to hide Your face,
Em   Bm/D   C
   I rest on Your   un-changing grace.
Em   Bm/E   G
   In every high and stormy gale,
Em   Bm/D   C   B B⁷
   My anchor holds   with-in the veil.